KNOW YOUR RIGHTS!

CONSUMER CREDIT REPORTING

DEBT HARASSMENT

Consumer Right to Compensation Simplified by:

California Consumer Trial Attorneys

Babak "Bob" Semnar, Esq. &

Jared Hartman, Esq.

Speakeasy Publishing
73-03 Bell Blvd, #10
Oakland Gardens, NY 11364
www.speakeasypublishinginc.com

Ordering Information:

Quantity sales. Special discounts are available on quantity purchases by corporations, associations, and others. For details, contact the publisher at the address above.

Orders by U.S. trade bookstores and wholesalers. Please contact Speakeasy Publishing: Tel: (888) 991-2766 or visit www.speakeasypublishinginc.com.

Printed in the United States of America.

Published in 2018.

ISBN: 978-1-946481-37-5

DEDICATION

This book is dedicated to all consumers who have been forced to contend with a Credit Bureau or financial institution due to inaccuracies on their credit reports or have experienced unlawful debt collection tactics.

# Acknowledgements

Although the contents of this book are derived from the personal experiences of the attorneys at Semnar & Hartman, LLP, the ability to share such experiences are made possible because of our immediate families, who take care of our personal commitments each and every day so that we may spend most of our time advocating for consumers.

We are also thankful for the men and women who have sacrificed their lives for our country so that we, as Americans, can coexist regardless of our race, religion, gender or sexual preference. Our society is a reflection of what service members and their families have sacrificed for, which in turn has resulted in a society that allows individuals to sue and seek monetary compensation from billion dollar companies within the context of debt harassment, credit reporting violations, and the rights of employees.

DISCLAIMER

This publication is intended to be used for educational purposes only. No legal advice is being given, and no attorney-client relationship is intended to be created by reading this material. The authors assume no liability for any errors or omissions, or for how this book and/or its contents are used or interpreted, or for any consequences resulting directly or indirectly from the use of this book. The content herein is based on statutes and court rulings as they exist at the time of writing, all of which is subject to change after publication of this book. The references to consumers throughout the book are made in the masculine; however, it is meant to include female and male consumers.

For legal or any other advice, please consult an experienced consumer attorney who can become aware of the specific facts of your case as it relates to law in your jurisdiction.

Semnar & Hartman LLP

41707 Winchester Road, Suite 201

Temecula, California 92590

(951) 293-4187

www.TemeculaConsumerAttorneys.Com

TESTIMONIALS

"Bob is an excellent attorney. He has helped me resolve issues that I had thought would never get fixed. He is extremely knowledgeable about consumer rights and really does fight for the little guy. After years of trying to fix multiple errors and dealing with collection agencies that didn't bother to follow the rules even when I did, Bob was able to get everything fixed for me and forced these companies to follow the law."

- Mary

****

"Jared is an exceptional Lawyer. He handled all aspects of our case providing very good advice. He knew what needed to be done and did it. Without his diligence and guidance throughout the process we would have been totally lost. I can honestly give him my highest recommendation."

- David

****

"A couple of minutes into my first phone conversation with Jared and Bob, I knew I found the right team. I felt like I was talking with family. They never sugar-coated anything, but I never felt scared or worried because I had so much confidence in their experience, knowledge of the law, and professionalism. I can confidently recommend Jared Hartman and Bob Semnar without hesitation and wish them continued success down the road."

- Anonymous

****

TABLE OF CONTENTS

- Dedication 3
- Acknowledgements 4
- Disclaimer 5
- Testimonials 6
- Personal Introductions 9
    - Bob Semnar 9
    - Jared Hartman 15

(Chapter 1) Consumer Law 20

- Types of Cases Involved 26
- Background Check Companies 27

(Chapter 2) General Life of a Consumer Law Case 29

- Time that Consumer Cases Typically Take 29
- Do Consumer Law Cases End Up Going to Trial? 30
- Outcome to Expect in Consumer Law Cases 31

(Chapter 3) Finding the Right Attorney 33

- Finding a Consumer Attorney 33
- Role of a Consumer Law Attorney 36
- Skills to Look for in an Attorney 37
- Can I Afford an Experienced Attorney? 39
- Impact of Experience, Reputation and Skill 40
- How Do I Know If It's Necessary to Hire a Consumer Law Attorney for My Case? 41

(Chapter 4) Credit Reporting Laws **42**

- Credit Reporting Errors 45
- Consequences of Credit Reporting Errors 47
- Steps to Take if You See Errors on Your Credit Report 49
- Fixing an Error on a Credit Report 50
- When to File a Lawsuit? 52
- Who to File a Lawsuit Against? 53

(Chapter 5) Factors that Make Up A High Value Consumer Law Case **55**

- Importance of Documented Evidence 59
- The Need to Act without Delay 61

(Chapter 6) The Problem with Most Credit Repair Companies **65**

(Chapter 7) Fair Debt Collection Practices Act **68**

A Message from Semnar & Hartman, LLP 71

- Index 73
- Notes 74

Personal Introductions

Babak "Bob" Semnar, Esq.

Mr. Babak "Bob" Semnar is passionate about representing individuals who have been wronged by big corporations. Since becoming an attorney in 2003, he has represented thousands of individuals, advocated for his clients hundreds of times in both in State and Federal Court, and has had over 30 jury trials. He takes great pride in obtaining maximum compensation for his clients. Since co-founding Semnar & Hartman, LLP in 2013, Mr. Semnar has regularly sued multi-million-dollar corporations on behalf of consumers for violations of FDCPA (Fair Debt Collection Practices Act), TCPA (Telephone Consumer Protection Act), as well as the FCRA (Fair Credit Reporting Act).

Personal Note from Babak "Bob" Semnar about his Connection to Consumer Law

Thank you for taking the time to read about me and my connection to consumer law. I am a first-generation immigrant from Iran. I left a country that was under the control of a dictator, to live in the United States. I came here in 1983 with my mother, my aunt, and my 3 cousins. Left behind was my father, who quickly lost interest in fulfilling his role as my father and proceeded to focus his attention on a new family.

Once we arrived in the United States, we were welcomed by my uncle, his family, and my grandparents. Growing up in America consisted of going to school during the day and working at nights in order to help with the bills. Although we were blessed to have the emotional and financial support of my uncle, my mom and I worked full time, while staying focused on my education.

Through the teaching of various family members, especially my uncle, who was my biggest fan, I learned the values associated with absolute kindness, giving without gaining anything in return, and the ability to silently lead.

Even as an attorney, I never forget the sacrifice that we have made to come here as first generation immigrants. I still recall the times that my mother and I lived in a two-bedroom apartment with my aunt, my three cousins, and my grandparents. My early years in the United States reinforced in me the values of family, conserving resources, and what it means to be a true working-class family. Our motivation and dedication for having a better life served to keep myself and my cousins in school, so that one day, we may elevate ourselves from working class into the middle class.

I lived in Northern California until my freshman year in High School. In 1992 I moved to Palm Springs for my sophomore year and then St. Monica's Catholic High School in Santa Monica for my junior and senior year, where I obtained my Diploma. At St. Monica's my ability to learn was supercharged, allowing me to significantly increase my reading and comprehension skills. My hard work allowed me to accepted at Loyal Marymount

University in Los Angeles. After obtaining my bachelor's degree I attended Whittier Law School in Costa Mesa, where I was introduced for the first time to trial advocacy and the art of making persuasive arguments on behalf of others. I graduated law school and passed the bar in 2003. After obtaining my license, I started working as an attorney, and I have been practicing law continuously since. I initially worked for an insurance defense firm where I learned how to defend civil cases. Then I moved to a plaintiff's personal injury firm, where I met hundreds of individuals who had sustained physical injuries due to the reckless and negligent conduct of others.

In 2005, while working as an attorney at The Law Offices of Robert W. Jackson in Fallbrook, I was introduced and accepted into Gerry Spence's Trial Lawyers College in Wyoming. My attendance at the college required me to live at their ranch in Wyoming, for three weeks with 50 other lawyers from around the country. During my time at the ranch, I worked on my trial skills from morning to night, every day, with the goal of better relating to my clients, their situation, their story and the justice that they deserve.

I graduated from the college in 2005 and have continued to work on my trial skills by working on my ability to better understand my clients. My teaching and training have not only made me a better lawyer in the Courtroom, but also a better person, friend, husband, and most importantly, a better father to my girls.

In 2006, I went back to Gerry Spence's Trial Lawyer's College and attended their graduate program. Immediately after, I started my own office with my cousin, who I viewed as an older brother, representing individuals who had been harmed due to their business/partnership dealings. We had our own firm from 2006 through 2008 when I joined the Riverside Public Defender's Office.

In 2008, as a public defender, I exclusively practiced criminal defense, representing individuals who were facing criminal charges but who could not afford an attorney. I handled cases involving a wide variety of crimes, some of which can only be described as despicable. I was also able to meet and continue to keep in touch with some clients, who are truly amazing people, who were simply going through a difficult time in their life. There my belief was confirmed that hurt, mistakes, emotions, anger, regret, as well as the desire to be kind is universal among ever class, every race, and every background. I had the privilege of serving as a public defender from 2008 to 2012.

In 2012, I started my own office called Semnar Law Firm, Inc. In 2013, I joined my friend and former public defender, Jared Hartman, to form a consumer law firm, Semnar & Hartman, LLP. Our firm represents consumers who have inaccurate information on their credit reports, who are being treated unfairly by debt collectors/creditors, or who have had their employment-related rights violated.

My experience as a first-generation immigrant, my moral values, as well as the education and training which I continue to obtain yearly, allow me to aggressively represent my clients without fear, and with complete confidence that I possess the foundation needed to advocate for my clients to the ultimate decider of the case, the jury of my client's peers.

Jared Hartman, Esq.

Mr. Hartman obtained his Bachelor's in Criminal Justice *cum laude* from Bowling Green State University, his Juris Doctorate *cum laude* from Cleveland-Marshall College of Law, and then the advanced and distinguished Master of Laws Degree in Criminal Law from the University of San Diego. Mr. Hartman was sworn to practice law in the State of California and ultimately obtained licensing to practice in all Federal Courts with jurisdiction in the State of California as well as the U.S. Court of Appeals for the Ninth Circuit.

During law school, Mr. Hartman was published for his legal research on Fourth Amendment issues involving high school students, and was also honored to be the recipient of the Charles Auerbach Outstanding Student in Evidence Award.

His courtroom experience and litigation has awarded him both an invitation into the National Trial Lawyers' Top 40 Under 40, reserved for the top 40 trial lawyers in each region under 40 years old who focus on criminal defense and plaintiffs' civil rights, and a Top Lawyer rating from Avvo.

Personal Note from Jared Hartman about his Connection to Consumer Law

I learned from an early age that many aspects of our society are slanted in favor of those in power—whether those in power be the government, the police, big corporations, or financial institutions. Like many middle-class families, I watched my parents toil and struggle time and time again to provide a decent life for me and my siblings, only to be taken advantage of and wronged time and time again.

My father was once fired from his job in middle management at a large retail company because he refused to fire someone who was subordinate to him when ordered by his superior who wanted the person fired for a personal vendetta. He thereafter became very active and involved in labor unions after gaining new employment with the U.S. Post Office. He also instilled in myself and my siblings the ethics of hard work and dedication to sticking up for "the little guy".

Later in my life, during college, I witnessed on the news riots in Cincinnati, where the lower-class minority community rioted for approximately 14 days over a long history of "justifiable" homicides at the hands of the police. Eventually, a teenager was shot and killed because the police claimed he was retrieving a firearm from his pocket, when he was actually reaching for his identification card. When the officers were cleared of wrongdoing, the community erupted into violent riots for approximately two weeks.

Witnessing injustices such as these ignited a passion in me to stick up for the little guy and to fight back against those who abuse their power. Knowing that regular, every day people are often outmatched in the legal system, I have dedicated my career to fighting the bullies in the courtroom.

Having gained invaluable courtroom experience as a Deputy Public Defender for the County of Riverside from 2008-2012, I have completed over 32 jury trials as of the time of this writing, and I take great pride in my legal research and persuasive writing abilities.

As a public defender, I was able to fight injustices in the criminal system on a daily basis, and there I learned vital courtroom skills and litigation skills that allow me to now be evenly matched with, if not better than, the lawyers who are paid large salaries to defend those in power. I also learned that the most powerful tool an individual can have against those in power is a public courtroom and a public jury trial, so that abuses of power and injustices can be brought to light and rectified through appropriate compensation via jury verdicts.

I now enjoy bringing these skills and this dedication to the table when dealing with corporate America and their lawyers, and am always eager to prosecute a case to jury trial so that those in power can learn what it means to have a jury of one's peers evaluate a company's wrongdoings.

CHAPTER 1
CONSUMER LAW

Consumer Law involves various areas, such as debt collection harassment, credit reporting rights, lemon law, product defect, false advertisement, and unfair business practices. Overall, it is a group of laws designed to provide consumers the ability to obtain relief against corporate America when they have been harmed. Consumer Law is generally designed to prevent businesses from engaging in fraudulent or unfair dealings at the cost of consumers.

As it relates to credit reporting violations, consumer law is an individual's right to seek damages for inaccurate information on their credit reports. It also includes a company's failure to reasonably investigate a dispute lodged by a consumer. Put simply, if an individual is harmed by false information on their credit report, a consumer has a right to seek monetary damages for the harm that was caused.

The harm caused usually comes about when someone attempts to use his credit report or his credit score to obtain credit or to apply for a job. Generally, by the time an individual realizes that he has false information on his credit reports, he has already been denied a loan, has received a higher interest rate than he should have, or has been denied a job. Typically, that's how a consumer is notified that he has been harmed and that he needs to talk to an attorney to help him 1) correct the false information, 2) evaluate the harm caused, and 3) pursue reimbursement for the financial harm that has been caused, to no fault of the consumer.

Debt collection harassment relates to the conduct of debt collectors or creditors who are attempting to collect a consumer debt. This can occur in many ways, but some of the more common scenarios involve communicating with a consumer in an inappropriate manner; such as calling the consumer too many times to where the volume of calls amounts to harassment; calling too early in the morning or too late at night; lying about the details of an alleged debt; informing friends, family, or employer about the debt; threatening the consumer with criminal action for failing to pay the debt; and claiming that the debt is still able to be pursued in court after the statute of limitations has expired. Other examples may include claiming that the debt is incurring interest or costs when it is not; misrepresentations about a violation of the law; and failing to provide consumer with required disclosures.

Debt harassment violations may entitle the consumer to statutory damages, actual damages by way of out of pocket loss, and emotional distress damages. The consumer is entitled to up to $1,000.00 in statutory damages under Federal Law, and up to $1,000.00 for willful violations under California state law. Even if the consumer is caused no actual out of pocket loss by the debt collector's conduct, the consumer is still allowed to seek statutory damages.

In addition to such statutory damages, the consumer has a right to seek actual damages. Actual damages include out of pocket loss, as well as emotional distress, such as being upset, losing sleep, crying, having a nervous breakdown, seeing a psychologist or needing time off from work.

Similarly, in the context of credit reporting, the consumer is entitled to statutory damages of up to $5,000.00 for each willful violation of California law, and up to $1,000.00 for willful violations of the federal law. Under federal law a consumer is also permitted to pursue punitive damages for willful violations.

Credit reporting violations also permit actual damages. For example, a consumer may notice on his credit report a debt collection account that does not belong to him. If that entry prevents the consumer from being provided a home loan in the amount of $350,000.00, then he could seek monetary recovery for the actual damages incurred. The actual damages could be the failure to obtain a loan, a higher interest rate for the loan, and the emotional harm caused.

Under the federal law, a claim for punitive damages allow the consumer to determine how much the defendants are worth, and then determine how much of a penalty it will take for the defendants to fix the problem so that it never occurs again. Punitive damages are generally capped only by how much the court may allow.

For example, if we were determining the appropriate amount of punitive damages to be assessed against Equifax for failing to keep a consumer's personal information private, we would consider how much Equifax's net worth is, and then what amount of penalty would properly prevent them from allowing such a harm to happen again. Then, we would consider the actual harm caused to the consumer as a factor in determining what is the appropriate amount of punitive damages to be assessed. Some Courts have used a 9 to 1 ratio as the limit, whereby the punitive damages are limited to 9 times the actual damages caused.

Ultimately, the most important aspect of punitive damages is that the consumer is given the power to obtain damages to punish the defendant and serve as an incentive to prevent the harm as a deterrent.

The other important aspect of both debt collection harassment and credit reporting violations is that the consumer who prevails after pursuing a lawsuit is entitled to recover the cost of attorney's fees, the cost of filing the lawsuit, the cost of experts, and other related costs associated with litigation, such as court filing fees, deposition costs, and even costs of copies used to prosecute the case.

The fact that the prevailing consumer is allowed to recover his litigation costs is essential in allowing this area of law to survive. This allows consumer attorneys to aggressively pursue on behalf of the consumer for the harm caused without ever having to charge the consumer any money. In most scenarios the cases are accepted by the attorney on a "contingency", which means the consumer attorney pays the costs up front and is only reimbursed after obtaining compensation for the consumer.

Types of Cases Involved

The most common cases that we handle are those involving debt collection harassment and inaccurate credit reporting. Debt collection harassment involves a consumer debt whereby either the original creditor or a third-party debt collector is trying to collect on an allegedly defaulted debt. If the debt is not legitimately owed, that fact by itself can be the basis for a lawsuit against the creditor or debt collector. Even if the debt is legitimately-owed, the consumer may still have a claim based on the way the creditor or debt collector is attempting to collect the debt.

Credit reporting cases involve inaccurate, false, incomplete, or misleading information on someone's consumer credit reports, such as where either a creditor or a credit bureau is reporting inaccurate information about an account. Even if the information is technically accurate, there can still be a violation of the credit reporting laws if the information is determined to be misleading or incomplete to such an extent that it could adversely impact credit applications. Once the consumer realizes that there is something wrong with the information on his credit report, that's generally when we get involved. We review the consumer's credit reports, identify the problem, attempt to remedy the situation, and ultimately seek monetary compensation for the harm that has been caused.

Background Check Companies

Generally, the defendants in a consumer credit reporting case are furnishers (such as the creditor or bank with whom the consumer has an account), or consumer credit reporting agencies (such as Experian, Equifax, or Trans Union).

Furnishers, such as banks and credit card companies, are the companies that provide information to the consumer credit bureaus about a consumer. Consumer credit reporting agencies are generally companies like Equifax, Trans Union and Experian, who take information from the furnishers and put that information on a consumer's credit report.

However, most people don't realize that the category of credit reporting companies such as Equifax, TransUnion and Experian also includes companies that conduct background checks for job applications. These companies are also considered credit reporting companies. Since they obtain information about individuals, accumulate it into a report, and give that report to potential employers, they are considered credit reporting agencies by statute.

As a result, background check companies are bound by the rules that protect consumers in credit reporting cases. This also means that they are bound by the damages that an individual can obtain from a credit reporting company, which includes actual damages, statutory damages, punitive damages, the costs of prosecuting the case and the costs of the attorney's fees.

If a consumer is not able to secure a job because of inaccurate information that has been reported by the background company to the potential employer, the consumer may be entitled to the income that they would have received from the potential employer, as well as statutory damages, punitive damages, as well as the costs of the lawsuit and reasonable attorneys' fees incurred.

CHAPTER 2
GENERAL LIFE OF A CONSUMER LAW CASE

Time that Consumer Cases Typically Take

On average, smaller cases take somewhere between 60 to 120 days to resolve. Cases that involve higher values of damages generally take longer.

In the consumer law setting, generally, the more the defendants fight and refuse to take responsibility for their wrong-doing, the more we must fight to prosecute these cases, which in turn means the value of the case grows higher because of an accumulation of attorneys' fees and costs. This means the longer the case takes before the defendant accepts responsibility, the more the attorneys are required to work to prepare and prosecute the case, which also means the attorneys will require more money from the defendant for their time. This also sometimes serves as a real incentive for defendants to conduct an early evaluation on the case so that the case can be resolved before the attorneys' fees and costs starts to drive the value of the case higher.

Do Consumer Law Cases End Up Going to Trial?

Consumer law cases usually do not go to trial. However, the risk of going to trial serves a real value in convincing defendants who otherwise would not take any responsibility for their conduct to do so early in the case.

Corporate defendants know that if the case goes to trial and they lose, the cost of pursuing a case and presenting it in front of a jury, from an attorney's fees perspective, can be astronomical. Additionally, a jury verdict is often 10 times the amount of what they would have to pay in settlement value. It serves a real purpose to be able to inform defense counsel that the consumer and his attorneys are prepared for trial, which means it is also important to be represented by an attorney who knows how to take a case to trial.

Just like everyone else, defendants do their research. If they know that a consumer lawyer is inexperienced in taking a case to trial, then they might refuse to settle the case knowing that they are going to push the consumer lawyer into an unfamiliar area. As a result, they won't offer the reasonable amount that they should to settle early in the case. In contrast, if they see that the consumer attorney is experienced with trials, and is willing to go to trial, the defendants are more likely to take responsibility early on and avoid the risk of losing at trial and having to be ordered to pay a judgment much greater than they otherwise could pay early in settlement.

Outcome to Expect in Consumer Law Cases

In the context of credit reporting, the expected outcome is usually to receive monetary compensation for the harm caused as well as potentially correcting the inaccurate information being reported, plus recovering attorneys' fees and costs.

In the context of debt collection harassment, the expected outcome is to obtain monetary compensation for the harm caused, and (if appropriate) waive the alleged debt, plus recovering attorneys' fees and costs.

CHAPTER 3
FINDING THE RIGHT ATTORNEY

Finding a Consumer Attorney

With the increased use of consumer review sites, an individual can find a good lawyer in 10 minutes. They can look at reviews that the attorney has on sites such as Yelp, AVVO, google-reviews, and even the attorney's own website. Review sites are easy to access and almost always free of charge. It is highly recommended that an individual takes the time to read the reviews available when searching for an attorney.

Most law firms have a website that describes the attorney's experience and what the attorney's reason is for believing that she or he is the best for the job. An individual should feel confident in going to a consumer lawyer, or any lawyer for that matter, and asking the tough questions as if it was a job interview. That's because it really is somewhat like a job interview for a job that the lawyer is trying to obtain.

The consumer should have no problem asking how many years the lawyer has been practicing, how many cases they have filed, how many times they have sued a defendant, and whether they have ever gone to trial. Most individuals think that all lawyers go to trial, but that is not the case. Approximately 90% of lawyers have never gone to trial, and many who have gone to trial have not gone enough times to develop and sharpen quality trial skills. It is vital for a potential client to know such information from his potential attorney.

Imagine looking for a brain surgeon, you would want to know if that surgeon has done other brain surgeries before going to them. The same applies for a lawyer. Make sure that when you speak to someone at the law firm, you talk to a lawyer, not a paralegal, law clerk or an assistant. Make sure that you can contact the lawyer after your meeting with additional questions, whether through email, cell phone calls or text messages. These are the things that our firm gives to our clients, which builds trust and confidence.

In some ways, engaging in potential or actual litigation is like going into a relationship with that law firm or that lawyer. You need to have a sense of connection with that individual. You need to feel they care about you, believe they understand you, feel comfortable and confident standing next to that individual in front of a courtroom full of jurors or a judge, and you must feel like they can advocate for you. You want them to be able to tell your story even when the other side is trying to derail it. The only way to do that is to speak to the lawyer on the phone or see them in person so that you can get a sense from them. Are they compassionate about you? Do they care about you? Are they willing to fight for you? If you get that sense from a lawyer, then you are in good hands. That's something an individual can use in evaluating any lawyer for any purpose, not just a consumer law lawyer.

Role of a Consumer Law Attorney

One role of a consumer law attorney is to counsel people and inform them of their rights. Most individuals don't know that debt collection harassment laws can protect them or that inaccurate credit reporting laws allow them to recover monetary damages. Another role of a consumer law attorney is to help the client pursue violations of these laws. Some of these laws require very specific steps to be taken before rights are triggered to protect and ultimately compensate the consumer.

A consumer attorney should take the proper steps to ensure that the client understands the law and knows what steps need to be taken for his rights to be protected. If necessary, the attorney's role is to represent the client to escalate the situation into formal litigation whereby the client can use the power of the courts to obtain the appropriate amount of monetary damages for the consumer. Sometimes that means facilitating a settlement, and sometimes that means preparing a case to be presented to a jury at trial.

Skills to Look for in an Attorney

Obviously, an attorney who seeks to represent consumers should be familiar with the law. Not all attorneys are educated in all areas of the law. Therefore, it is generally recommended that a consumer-related case be handled by an attorney who has dedicated his practice to focus on consumer rights.

A consumer attorney will most likely have regular exposure to the technical nuances that sometimes prevent consumers from being able to fully take advantage of the laws that are in place to protect their interests. Unfortunately, the number one goal for a corporate defendant usually is attempting to avoid liability by taking advantage of failures of the consumer in following strict and technical compliance of the various prerequisite steps in hopes of eliminating the consumer's ability to be fully compensated and fully protected.

A consumer attorney should know of, and be prepared for, technical defense strategies and know how to avoid them. An attorney should inform the consumer about potential pitfalls and lead them to a position where no technical flaws exist, leaving the defense to have no other choice but to address the consumer's case on its merits and value.

It is significantly helpful if the attorney has previously represented clients at trial. If a lawyer doesn't regularly go to trial or has not had any real experience in prosecuting cases to trial, then they are ultimately at a serious disadvantage, as they lack the experience to know what to do if the case is not able to be settled before trial. An attorney who lacks the knowledge and experience to go to trial is no different than a gun that lacks bullets—the unloaded gun gives the impression to others that it could cause harm, but without bullets, it lacks the necessary ability to complete the job that it was assigned to do.

The ability to prepare a client's case and ultimately present the case at trial are things that both Mr. Semnar and Mr. Hartman bring to the table. We not only know how to prosecute a case to the end, but we look forward to it. We have each completed over 30 trials, which means that we are familiar with what it takes to prepare a case, what constitutes admissible evidence, how to present the evidence at trial, how to argue trial motions and objections in front of the judge, and, most importantly, how to persuasively present our client's story to a jury.

Until you have repeatedly represented a client before a jury, you will not appreciate the value and power that a jury trial has in resolving a dispute in litigation. After repeated trials, we know that a trial before members of the community is sometimes the most powerful weapon that a consumer has against corporate America. It is the consumer's peers that can, and most times do, hold corporations responsible for taking advantage of consumers and refusing to take responsibility for the harms they have caused. It is for this reason that an effective consumer attorney must also be a trial attorney; otherwise, they are seriously putting their client at a disadvantage.

Can I Afford an Experienced Attorney?

In the majority of cases, experienced consumer law firms pay for all the costs and fees associated with the lawsuit (including hiring experts, funding depositions, traveling to different states to take depositions and presenting a case to trial) without charging the client anything up front. So, the answer is almost always yes. In such "contingency" fee cases, the attorney is only paid for his time and reimbursed his out of pocket costs if the litigation results in a successful recovery.

Impact of Experience, Reputation and Skill

We look at every lawsuit like a chess match. We evaluate the defense firms, evaluate the defense attorneys, and rank their ability to persuasively present a defense.

We presume that the defendants are doing the exact same thing by evaluating our firm. They are evaluating the way we have prosecuted cases in the past and evaluating our ability to pursue the lawsuit all the way to a jury trial. It's a huge factor that plays into cases that is not acknowledged but considered when it comes to negotiations. Defense attorneys won't admit, "I'm settling the case with you because I know you'll pursue the case to trial." However, it's common sense that they are taking such a factor into consideration.

In fact, Mr. Semnar used to work for insurance defense firms defending personal injury cases, and he learned that the considerations by the defense industry always involved evaluating the lawyer representing the plaintiff, including their ability to prosecute the case to trial.

A good trial lawyer would get a higher value settlement than a lawyer that clearly didn't have the experience or the ability to pursue the case to trial.

How Do I Know If It's Necessary to Hire a Consumer Law Attorney for My Case?

You might discover that it's necessary when you yourself try to send a written dispute asking the credit reporting agencies or the furnishers to correct an error and they refuse to do so or simply ignore you. In such circumstances, you might feel lost and helpless as to what else could be done to protect yourself and assert your rights. Therefore, it is advisable to seek the assistance of an attorney from the very beginning. This is because you want somebody who is navigating the laws and pitfalls in the right way. You want somebody who is going to stand by you if the companies ignore you, and you want somebody who is going to seek monetary damages for you if your requests are ignored or mishandled.

CHAPTER 4
CREDIT REPORTING LAWS

Consumers who reside in California have the protection of both the California Consumer Credit Reporting Agencies Act as well as the Federal Fair Credit Reporting Act. The California Consumer Credit Reporting Agencies Act starts at Civil Code Section 1785, while the Federal Fair Credit Reporting Act can be found at 15 United States Code Section 1681 (15 U.S.C. 1681).

In essence, the California Act is equivalent to the Federal Fair Credit Reporting Act with the exception that you have more rights under the California Act. Under

California Law, a consumer can file a lawsuit against the company that provides inaccurate, incomplete, or misleading information on the consumer's credit report without having to first file an informal dispute of the false information. This is a course of conduct that does not exist under the Federal Fair Credit Reporting Act.

Under the Federal Fair Credit Reporting Act, you must first file a written dispute with the consumer credit reporting agencies (Equifax, TransUnion or Experian) to trigger protections under the federal law. You must explain to them what is inaccurate on your credit report and why you think it needs to be removed or corrected, and you must provide sufficient information in your dispute to allow them to conduct an investigation into why the information should be corrected or removed. Under federal law, they have 30 days to investigate your dispute and remedy the situation. If they don't properly investigate or remedy it, or if they improperly reject your dispute, then you can sue them under the federal law.

Consider the following scenario: you are dealing with Equifax and Wells Fargo. If Wells Fargo reports wrong information on your credit report, then according to the federal law, you must first file a written dispute to Equifax telling them why the information that Wells Fargo is reporting on your credit report is inaccurate. Equifax then has 5 business days to contact Wells Fargo to inform them of the dispute, and both companies have 30 days from the date Equifax received the dispute to determine if the information should be changed or deleted, and then inform you of the results of the investigation.

After those 30 days you can move forward under the federal law to sue either (or both) Equifax or Wells Fargo for not investigating properly, not investigating within the statutory time allowed, or improperly rejecting the dispute. Under the California Act, that process doesn't need to exist with respect to a lawsuit against Wells Fargo. This is because you can sue Wells Fargo without ever writing a dispute to Equifax first.

This is when a consumer attorney can help to evaluate the situation to determine whether you should sue the creditor directly under only the California Act, or if you would prefer to instead file the written dispute to allow the dispute process to play out. This might be because you cannot determine if the inaccurate reporting truly is the fault of the creditor or the credit reporting agency, and we prefer to trigger the dispute process to help provide us with that information; or it might be that we prefer to file the lawsuit in federal court as opposed to state court; or it might be that we prefer federal statutory and punitive damages. Each case is different, so each case requires its own analysis and determination of strategy.

Credit Reporting Errors

Credit reporting errors are very common. A special investigative episode was conducted by "20/20", and they found that one out of every three individuals in the United States has inaccurate information on their credit reports. Individuals simply don't check their credit reports enough, and when they do, they don't catch the inaccuracies or don't know how to address them properly. Some inaccuracies are not blatant or easy to catch, but they affect your credit score nonetheless.

For example, some of the nuanced inaccuracies would be reporting a higher balance on your credit report than what you really owe, which might impact your debt-to-income ratio, or reporting the default date of an account as more recently than what the actual default was, which impacts the credit score because more recent defaults are scored more negatively than older defaults.

A more recent default account has more weight against your credit score than an older default account. If you fell behind on your loan last month, that's going to have a more significant effect on your credit report than if you fell behind five years ago.

Sometimes creditors will change the default date to make it appear more recent to increase the pressure on the consumer to pay that debt in full. But sometimes it's subtler than that. For example, it could be reported as being one or two years more recent than it is, which could affect the consumer's ability to move forward with a new loan. The consumer might say, "This account is legitimately mine and I didn't pay for it," but they won't realize that the default date or the balance has been changed in a way that negatively affects them.

Consequences of Credit Reporting Errors

Credit reporting issues can be very serious because people usually don't look at their credit reports until they need to. It's usually done at the last stages of moving forward with a new loan or credit application. For example, someone may find a home and obtain pre-qualification for a loan, only to find out at the last minute that they have a debt collection account that they otherwise were not aware of. At that point, the consumer is under a time constraint because he is already in escrow, and the ability to eliminate that information from the credit report is really the difference between buying the house and not buying the house.

The other way consequences come into play is when people apply for jobs. A lot of employers request credit reports, and oftentimes the employer won't even tell the applicant that he did not get the job because of something on his credit report. As a result, the individual doesn't even know it's affecting him. That's a serious consequence. It can have a significant impact because it comes at such a critical part in an individual's life, in that it makes all the difference between obtaining employment or not.

Depending on the conduct of the debt collector, debt collection harassment issues can also have a significant impact. If the consumer is experiencing egregious conduct from a debt collector, it could cause significant emotional distress, such as anxiety, worry, loss of sleep, depression, inability to focus at work, and even arguments within their marriage. Oftentimes, people are scared to be in their own house because of threats they have received, and they may believe that someone is going to come looking for them to either commit violence, serve them with legal process, or have law enforcement arrest them if they do not pay. Such threats are completely inappropriate and illegal in California.

Steps to Take if You See Errors on Your Credit Report

If you find an inaccuracy on your credit report, the first thing you should do is call a consumer law attorney. Most lawyers out there who do consumer law will provide a free consultation to the individual, review the credit reports, and tell him what information needs to be gathered to protect his rights. It's a free service, and pretty much every attorney offers it. If an attorney does not offer such a free service, then don't consult with that attorney.

It's worth every moment of your time to speak to a consumer attorney, because every piece of information on a credit report is different, and the documentation needed to protect your rights comes with different strategies depending on each particular scenario. There is not a blanket solution for every scenario. So, your number one goal should be to talk to a consumer attorney.

The next step would be to gather the documents that show the inaccuracy. Most of the time an inaccuracy will show that you owe some amount of money when you in fact do not. You can substantiate your dispute with documents, such as proof that the debt had already been paid. If it's something that you don't have any documentation for, like an account on your credit report that you've never had, then you can contact the company that is reporting that information and ask for documented proof. Any time you contact a company, you should always contact them in writing, via certified mail, and request records to substantiate the information. Contacting them in writing via certified mail is your best proof that you contacted them, and you should always keep a copy of the letter you sent them.

Fixing an Error on a Credit Report

In theory, inaccurate information on someone's credit reports should be easy to fix. The consumer files his dispute in writing, delivers the letter to the credit reporting agencies, and the credit reporting agencies forward the dispute to the furnisher (which is the company that's providing the information to the credit reporting agencies). The furnisher then looks at their records, realizes it's inaccurate, and tells the credit reporting agencies to delete the information or correct the error. In theory, that's how it's supposed to work; it should be relatively easy.

Unfortunately, a practical reality is that it's not always so easy. This is because the credit reporting agencies usually don't have a proper system in place to deal with the high volume of disputes that they receive.

In addition, the furnishers often don't have the right personnel in place to properly investigate such disputes. So, instead of looking into consumer disputes, they would rather just say, "This is accurate. We validate this information." and then move on. Because the process is much more complicated in reality than what it should be, it's worthwhile to have a consumer attorney on your side. A consumer attorney will ensure that things are done properly the first time, and if it doesn't get done correctly, then the consumer attorney will have the right tools to move to the next stage, which may be litigation.

When to File a Lawsuit?

Under the Federal Fair Credit Reporting Act, you must file a dispute and wait 30 days to receive the results. Once the 30 days are up, you can file your lawsuit and seek the damages that have been caused. Under the California Act, if you believe the furnisher (such as Wells Fargo or Bank of America) either knew or should have known of the inaccuracy at the time of reporting the information, then you can file a lawsuit the moment you see it on your credit report and seek damages to make yourself whole for the inaccuracy.

As discussed more below, it is vital to act quickly under either scenario, because the statute of limitations is a very strict deadline that prevents you from being able to file suit if not met. Under either the Federal or the California Act, the statute of limitations is the sooner of either 7 years from the date of the violation by the company involved, or 2 years from the date the consumer either knew or should have known of the violation.

This means that, if you file a lawsuit, and the company can prove that you obtained your credit report more than 2 years before filing the lawsuit, and you therefore should have known of the violation more than 2 years prior to filing suit, then your case could be lost on summary judgment or dismissed with prejudice. Therefore, as soon as you discover a violation, you must contact a consumer attorney right away to understand what your rights are and what is the best strategy on how to proceed further.

Who to File a Lawsuit Against?

Under the Fair Credit Reporting Act, you can sue the credit reporting agencies (Equifax, TransUnion and Experian) for not properly investigating your disputes, not timely investigating, or mishandling the disputes. Under the federal law, once the 30-day dispute period is up, you may also sue the furnisher (Wells Fargo, Bank of America, Citibank, Chase and debt collectors who report information on credit reports) for also not properly investigating your disputes, not timely investigating, or mishandling the disputes.

In some cases, it is also possible to sue the credit reporting agencies under the federal law without first lodging a dispute, if you can prove that they failed to follow proper procedures to ensure maximum possible accuracy upon preparing a report in the first place. Such a claim is usually difficult to prove, and it does not exist as against the furnishers of information. As such, it is usually more advisable to follow the dispute procedures to assert a federal claim under both theories.

CHAPTER 5
FACTORS THAT MAKE UP A HIGH VALUE CONSUMER LAW CASE

Consumer cases are often valued by looking at the way they've affected the consumer. We usually start by considering how egregious the conduct was; meaning, how many times did the conduct occur, over what period, how easily could it have been fixed or prevented, and how often did the consumer informally request the company to fix the problem. Then, we consider how the violation affected the individual and what are the circumstances surrounding that individual. The same conduct can have different effects on different individuals. For example, a case in which someone already has a job and is prevented from getting a better job because of something on their credit report might have a lower value than a case in which somebody needs a job to avoid eviction.

Once a violation is identified in a consumer credit reporting case, or a debt collection harassment case, we can either seek to remedy the problem through pre-litigation communication with the violator or, in some cases, immediately commence litigation. Unfortunately, in most circumstances, it is most productive to fix the problem caused to the consumer while the case is simultaneously being prosecuted. This is because companies often disregard or ignore efforts to fix the problem pre-litigation, and they only start to show concern for fixing the problem once they must start paying legal fees to defend the lawsuit. Also, once the case has commenced, attorneys' fees and costs increase significantly, which may add additional value to the case.

An example of a high value case is one where the consumer is trying to do something with his credit report, such as buy a home, get a car, or obtain a job, but is not able to do so because of the inaccurate information on his credit report.

If the consumer is not able to obtain a job, a car loan, or a home loan, the damages incurred are generally substantial and serve as the basis for a higher value settlement. If someone lost his job, the income and benefits lost would become part of the damages. If someone couldn't obtain the home he wanted, then the lack of ability to move into that home would be what we pursue as part of the damages. So, the value changes depending on what the person was trying to do with his credit report and what he was not able to do because of the inaccurate information contained in the credit report.

It's also important to note that a direct "but-for" cause and effect is not required. Sometimes, that's one of the tricks defendants may pull. They often say, "You can't prove that's a direct link for why your client did not get the loan or did not get hired by a potential employer." Other times they will ask, "How do you know which debt collection account that was found on your client's credit report was the basis for the denial of the loan or the job? How do you know it wasn't caused by the other debt collection accounts that are legitimately on your client's credit report?" These are routine defenses that are claimed in credit reporting cases as a means of avoiding responsibility for reporting inaccurate information on a consumer's credit report.

In response to such claims by defendants it is important to point out that they either are misinformed of the standard of proof, or they are playing ignorant of the standard to obtain an improper advantage. The premise of such defense is that there is no direct link between the wrong information reported and the caused injury to the consumer. Simply put, this is legally the wrong standard to be applied.

In actuality, the standard of proof between the inaccurate information contained on a consumer's credit report and the wrong that resulted is a "substantial factor test" and not a direct link "but-for" test. This means if the inaccurate information is simply a "substantial factor" in causing the harm (i.e. preventing the person from getting the home or the car or the job), then the consumer has met his burden, and the company that put the inaccurate information on his credit report is responsible for the damages caused.

The courts have recognized that, in a credit reporting case, it is almost impossible to directly link any single inaccuracy to a result or harm under a "but-for" test. Therefore, in a consumer credit reporting case, the consumer must only show the inaccuracy on his credit report was a substantial factor to the harm caused.

Importance of Documented Evidence

Unfortunately, what may seem to be obvious facts today will often be "selectively" lost or forgotten when the information is needed to hold defendants responsible, and unfortunately it is common for defendants to "purge their files" on a routine basis and thereby deprive us from obtaining necessary documentation via subpoena or formal discovery. Therefore, it is critical that consumers take the extra step to document their specific situations.

With respect to credit reporting violations, it is necessary to regularly pull and save your credit reports. This is the easiest way to preserve evidence. In the context of interacting with credit reporting agencies or creditors, do not accept mere verbal discussions with their employees; get it in writing. We have often run into the problem that the debt collector or creditor has "purged" or "lost" recorded phone conversations that might prove our case against them. However, if the communication is done in writing, even via e-mail, then your own record of the communication cannot be "lost" or "purged" by the company.

In current times, virtually everybody has a cell phone and an email account. So, if somebody tells you that you are not going to get a loan because of something on your credit report, ask them to send you an email. If they won't send it to you, send them an email confirming what they just told you so that it becomes documented and time-stamped. Even if they do not respond to your email, at least you have a documented record of confirming what they told you.

The same applies for debt collection harassment cases. If someone curses at you, harasses you, calls you names, or tells you lies or false threats, then you are likely not going to be to get an email from that person admitting, "I just called and harassed you." However, you can write an email to that company explaining what just happened so that it is a documented record of what you just experienced. And if the company does happen to respond to apologize for the conduct, then we might have a legal admission that can be used as evidence in the lawsuit.

If no email address can be found for the employee who is communicating with the consumer, it is recommended that the consumer email himself and memorialize what occurred, as if creating a diary entry. This again will allow the consumer to document the events as they just occurred in a safe and secure place, time stamped to be used later, if needed.

The Need to Act without Delay

A factor that can take a high-valued case to no value in an instant is the failure on the part of the consumer to act quickly. As discussed above, once the consumer is on notice that there exists information on his credit report that is not accurate, he is legally obligated to act within a certain time or be faced with having his right to do so waived. The time that the consumer must act is called the statute of limitations.

The statute of limitations for both the state and federal credit reporting laws are two years from the time the violation was discovered by the consumer (or reasonably should have been discovered) or seven years from the time it occurred - whichever comes first.

The two-year time starts to run from the time that the consumer knows or should have known of the violation. The seven-year time starts from the time that the violation first occurred. Whichever event comes first will foreclose the consumer from pursuing legal action.

So, if there is an inaccuracy on the consumer's credit report that he didn't know about until after the fourth year, then he would have two years from the time that this information was discovered by the consumer to pursue the case.

If, however, there is inaccurate information on a consumer's credit report that he didn't know about until after 10 years, and then this information is known, the statute of limitation would have already passed and the consumer would be legally prevented from pursing his rights under either the Federal or State Credit Reporting Acts.

In some instances, there are ways that the Statute of Limitations can be renewed. Under the Federal Fair Credit Reporting Act (FCRA), a consumer can submit a written dispute to fix or remove an item on his/her credit report. Some courts have found that the consumer's dispute serves to trigger a new violation through a reinvestigation requirement on behalf of the companies involved, and as such, a new two-year statute of limitations begins on its own independently of any prior statute of limitations. Under this theory, it can be argued that if the credit reporting agencies don't properly reinvestigate the new consumer dispute, then that could be a new and separate violation that would have its statute of limitations.

It is very important to know, however, that under debt collection harassment laws, the statute of limitations is one year from the time that the harassment occurs, whether that harassment is in the form of a phone call or a letter. There are dozens of ways that a debt collector or creditor can violate debt collection harassment laws, any one of which can be a basis for commencing a lawsuit against them. However, the statute of limitations for the wrong committed is one year from the time it occurred.

If the violation is one that could not reasonably have been discovered by the consumer within one year of the violation occurring (such as being sued in an improper judicial venue and not being served for two years), then the consumer can argue that the statute of limitations did not even begin until the violation was discovered or reasonably should have been discovered. But this "discovery rule" is not a guarantee in any lawsuit, which means the consumer must act right away by contacting a consumer attorney upon first discovering any conduct that might be considered a violation of the debt collection harassment laws.

CHAPTER 6
THE PROBLEM WITH MOST CREDIT REPAIR COMPANIES

Many consumers ask if they should hire a "credit repair" company to help them attempt to lodge disputes to the credit bureaus. Unfortunately, we have spoken to many consumers who have been severely harmed by these companies that claim to have their best interests in mind. In fact, most will promise a result that is practically impossible. They will claim to have some secret formula that allows them to essentially make your credit report perfect, when that claim is very far from the truth.

Generally, credit repair companies will write disputes on behalf of the individual and charge the individual a monthly fee to continuously write monthly disputes to the credit bureaus, with the basis of the disputes often drastically changing from one letter to the next. Unfortunately, most credit repair companies write disputes that are not accurate, meaning they will just frivolously claim that the account is showing a wrong balance, is not the individual's account, has already been settled, or was supposed to have been deleted. They lodge so many frivolous disputes with the hope that the credit reporting agencies will delete the information instead of investigating the numerous disputes. Many times, this strategy is implemented without the consumer's knowledge or authorization, even though each letter is submitted on behalf of the consumer in his name.

Such a circumstance creates a long-documented history of false disputes in the consumer's name, which means if the consumer ever does have a need to pursue legal action over a legitimate dispute, then the defendants might be able to defend the lawsuit by claiming that all disputes from this consumer are frivolous, and therefore they were justified in ignoring even the legitimate disputes. Such a circumstance could also render the consumer as being unbelievable and discreditable, which means any information that the consumer must give through undocumented testimony could be treated with suspicion and lack of trust. Either way, the consumer has been severely (and potentially, permanently) harmed in any future dealings and legal actions with the companies involved.

More importantly, these credit repair companies don't provide a means for the individual to take it to the next step of litigation if the disputes are mishandled. If the credit reporting agencies violate the Credit Reporting Acts in some way, the credit repair companies will just send more dispute letters instead of initiating litigation. That doesn't do anything for the individual except make them wait even longer for a hopeful correction that may never come.

In contrast, a consumer attorney could file a lawsuit if the inaccuracy was falsely validated even once. Once a lawsuit is filed, the individual would have the ability to not only eventually have the inaccurate information fixed, but also to seek monetary compensation.

CHAPTER 7
FAIR DEBT COLLECTION PRACTICES ACT

The Federal Fair Debt Collection Practice Act deals with harassing conduct by third party debt collectors, meaning a company who did not initiate the debt in the first place. The equivalent to that in California is the Rosenthal Act, which addresses conduct by third party debt collectors as well as the original creditors who are collecting on their own consumer debts.

The primary difference between the California Fair Debt Collection Practice Act (also called the Rosenthal Act) and the Federal Fair Debt Collection Practice Act is that the former allows you to hold responsible both the original creditor and the debt collector, while the latter only allows you to hold the third-party debt collector responsible.

A creditor is the company that entered into the initial transaction with the consumer and gave the consumer something on credit. If a creditor is unable to collect the balance owed from the consumer and sells their account to a third-party, then that third-party may be considered the debt-collector because they are now in a position to collect on the debt and they did not engage in the initial dealings with the consumer.

Consumer debts are those that are incurred for personal or household purposes; a business debt does not qualify under either Act. If the collector or creditor pursues the debt in a manner that's illegal (of which there are approximately 42 different ways) then it's a strict liability offense, which means it doesn't matter if they had good intentions or bad intentions. If they are found liable, they must pay the consumer statutory damages, actual damages, attorney's fees and the cost of the lawsuit.

Moreover, under the California law, the original transaction must be a "credit transaction", whereas under the federal law it doesn't matter if it's a credit transaction or not. For example, a credit card bill is a credit transaction because the credit card company allows the consumer to spend money on credit ahead of time and then the consumer pays the credit used back over time. If it was a simultaneous event - meaning you bought and paid for something at the same time - it would not be considered a credit transaction and would not qualify under the California Rosenthal Act

A MESSAGE FROM:

SEMNAR & HARTMAN
LLP

At Semnar & Hartman, LLP, there is no consultation fee and no obligation to sign up. We provide everyone with a free and confidential evaluation of their case. There is no reason why a person shouldn't call a consumer law firm like ours. At the very minimum, people who consult with us gain more information than they had before. More importantly, if a lawsuit is filed, the fees that are incurred (the attorney's time, the litigation costs, the expert fees, the deposition fees etc.) may be recoverable in the lawsuit.

Our office is located in Temecula, CA. However, we are always available to speak to any potential client over the phone at (951) 293-4187. More detailed information about the topics discussed in this book can be found on our website:

www.TemeculaConsumerAttorneys.com

INDEX

C

CALIFORNIA FAIR CREDIT REPORTING ACT · 42

CONSUMER LAW · 21

CONSUMER LAW ATTORNEY · 36

CREDIT REPAIR COMPANY · 66

CREDIT REPORTING · 21

CREDIT REPORTING ERRORS · 45

D

DEBT HARASSMENT · 21

DEFENDANTS · 30

DEPOSITIONS · 39

F

FEDERAL FAIR CREDIT REPORTING ACT · 42

J

JURY VERDICT · 30

S

STATUTE OF LIMITATIONS · 62

NOTES